SONGS OF LOVE AND WAR

SONGS OF LOVE AND WAR

AFGHAN WOMEN'S POETRY

———

Sayd Bahodine Majrouh

translated from the Pashtun into French,
adapted and introduced
by André Velter and the author

translated from the French
by Marjolijn de Jager

OTHER

Other Press • New York

Originally published as *Le suicide et le chant: poésie populaire des femmes pachtounes.* Copyright © Editions Gallimard, Paris, 1994.

Translation copyright © 2003 Marjolijn de Jager

Production Editor: Robert D. Hack

This book was set in 12.5 pt. Garamond by Alpha Graphics of Pittsfield, NH.

10 9 8 7 6 5 4 3 2 1

Library of Congress Cataloging-in-Publication Data

Majruh, Baha al-Din, 1928–
  [Suicide et le chant. English]
  Songs of love and war : Afghan women's poetry / Sayd Bahodine Majrouh ; translated from the Pashtun into French, adapted and introduced by André Velter and the author ; translated from the French by Marjolijn de Jager.
      p. cm.
Translated from French.
  ISBN 1–59051–081–X (alk. pbk.)
  1. Pushto poetry–Women authors–Translations into English. 2. Women–Afghanistan–Social conditions–Poetry. I. De Jager, Marjolijn. II. Velter, André. III. Title.

PK6819.M35A26 2003
891'.59310809287–dc21

2003013367

Introduction   ix

I   1

II   11

III   19

Forty Landays   25

IV   37

Ninety-Three Landays of Exile   51

Afterword   73

When he arrived, it had all been played out.
The turmoil had abated. The crowd was slowly
breaking up.

To one side stood a few religious dignitaries with
somber beards, their turbans and black robes
enveloping them in an aura even more funereal
than usual.

The Voyager reached the center of the square.
Half buried beneath a mound of stones lay a young
woman and a young man, covered in mud and blood.

Sayd Bahodine Majrouh
Le rire des amants (*Lovers' Laughter*)

INTRODUCTION

WITHOUT ANY MODELS to emulate, without any poetic authorities to respect, the authors of oral literature in the Pashtun language create their work at a far remove from any books. Generally deprived of the support of school or university, they protect their compositions from outside influences and spontaneously give their work the power of characteristic echoes through which an entire people can be heard.

Nevertheless, these popular improvisations have managed to develop forms of great diversity with very specific rules of versification. Inseparable from song, such poetry is not meant to be recited. More than anything else, its rhyme and rhythm have melodic value.

In terms of content, it is clearly different from Persian *dari* poetry. It does not exalt mystic love. There is no yearning whatsoever here for an unknown, unfathomable, and incommunicable heaven. Nor is it devoted to praising the lord. No image appears of an absolute master who holds the life and death of his subjects in his hands. The portrait of an Adonis, the object of homosexual desire, is totally absent as well. Wordplay, elegance of feelings, metaphoric preciosity—rhetorical exercises that Persian literature sometimes pushes to absurd limits—are not expressed either.

On the other hand, something simple and very basic is constantly affirmed here. The song of an earthly human being with its concerns, worries, joys, and pleasures; a song that celebrates nature, mountains, valleys, forests, rivers, dawn and dusk, and night's magnetic space; a song that feeds on war and honor, too, on shame and love, on beauty and death.

However, the great originality of this popular poetry is the active presence of woman. If, as everywhere else, she is the inspiration for male poets, here she imposes herself above all as creator, as the author and subject of innumerable songs. Thus, one form always requires her participation and this is the *landay,* which literally means "the short one." It is, indeed, a very brief poem consisting of two verse lines of nine and thirteen syllables respectively, without any obligatory rhyme but with solid internal scansions. Depending on the region, it is vocalized in different ways and frequently punctuates conversations where it is used as a quote or a saying, lending support to a feeling or an idea.

Like a cry coming from the heart, a lightning flash, a flame, the *landay* captures the attention by its brevity and rhythm. Furthermore, this anonymous poetry stands out because of its almost timeless emulation. Every afternoon, when village girls go to get water from the spring or when they dance and sing at a celebration or a wedding, new *landays* are improvised and the best ones then immediately become anchored in the collective memory.

Every man or woman is thus able to give voice to an emotion, a desire, or a lament through the two sung verse lines. Yet, grammatical form as much as inspiration helps to differentiate the various creators. People of letters and clerics use erudite terms,

Koranic allusions, and Persian or even Arabic expressions—their compositions reek of artifice. In contrast, the cantors without literary and religious education bear witness to greater vigor and little artifice even if their melodies only rarely attain the profound and pure restraint of the women's *landay*. Indeed, the latter springs from that part of the community that is maliciously left uncultivated. If they are simple and frail, as beautiful as the wild flowers of the surrounding plains and mountains, it is because they are born without having been sown in orderly fashion, they are unprotected and without any affectation. In a strict sense, they exist offscreen—off the cultural screen that is reserved exclusively for men and, consequently, off the social screen. The feelings and ideas they convey, however, leave absolutely no doubt as to the gender of their authors: a Pashtun man could not evoke some of the intrigues, even as a parody. For example, it is psychologically impossible for him to present a lover whose virility has been challenged or whose dignity humiliated.

Therefore, all the *landays* presented in this study originated from the female compendium in which the authenticity of tone is revealed to be incomparable. For it is a fascinating face that emerges from these texts in which women sing and speak about themselves, about men, and about the world around them. Theirs is a proud and merciless face that is in rebellion.

In the Pashtun community, with its tribal and clannish structure, women's condition is especially difficult. In a group of warriors of which only the adult men who belong to the tribe and sub-clans are fully fledged members, the society is run entirely by male values with the code of honor as its fundamental law. In such an environment, masculinized to the extreme, pious and fanatic in its own way, women are subjected to a double physical and moral oppression.

Physically, they shoulder the weight of the most exhausting domestic tasks. If from time to time the men exchange gunshots and occasionally work in the fields, the better part of their life is spent in the mosque or the village square—places where affairs of tribal policy are discussed. Women, on the other hand, work throughout the year from well before dawn until deep into the night. In addition to the help they provide during the harvest season, they assume regular and permanent manual labor without rest or any time off. At least twice a day, morning and evening, the woman goes to get water from the spring or river, sometimes traveling long distances with very heavy containers on her head or in her arms. She takes care of the children—always in large numbers—the cooking, and the cattle; she grinds meal, prepares flour, bakes bread, weaves wool, sews clothes, dries animal manure, and irrigates the crops. Yet, these women never bemoan their slave labor. Rare are the *landays* in which they mention their "velvet fingers" that gather the kernels of wheat or the all too heavy jars that make their backs ache.

In fact, what causes most of their suffering is the moral side of their subjugation. They feel repressed, scorned, and thought of as second rate human beings. From the cradle on, they are received with sadness and shame—shame that does not spare the mother who gives birth to a daughter. The father who learns of such an unwelcome arrival seems to go into mourning, whereas he gives a party and fires off a salvo of gunshots at the birth of a boy. Later, and without ever being consulted, the little girl becomes monetary exchange between families of the same clan. She spends her entire life in a state of inferiority, subordination, and humiliation. Even her husband does not stoop so low as to eat with her.

In the face of such conditions, of such ancestral restraints, what could her reaction be? Apparently, it is total submission. She performs her duties like clockwork. She accepts and suffers the value system that makes her just an object among so many others. And yet, if one takes a slightly closer look, it turns out that in her innermost self the Pashtun woman is indignant and skeptical, feeding her rebellion. From this deep-seated and hidden protest that grows more resistant with every passing day, she comes out with only two forms of evidence in the end—her suicide and her song.

It is known that the tribal code of honor considers suicide a cowardly act and that Islam forbids it. A Pashtun male never resorts to it. By eliminating herself in such an accursed way, a woman thus tragically proclaims her hatred of the community's law. Even her choice of the means by which to die emphasizes the iconoclastic meaning of the sacrifice: it is made only with poison or deliberate drowning. There is no bullet wound to the heart, no hanging, since the tools needed—rifle or rope—touch the execrated hands far too closely. Man uses the rifle to hunt and wage war and he uses rope to tie up cattle and branches of wood or to pull heavy loads.

If with her suicide the Pashtun woman forces a socially irremediable act upon her community, her song creates a challenge of a similar nature that in its own way can also prove to be fatal to her, because her melodies tirelessly glorify three themes that taste of blood. They are the themes of love, honor, and death.

I

A WOMAN'S LOVE is taboo, banned by the prohibition of the honor code of Pashtun life and by religious sentiment. Young people do not have the right to see each other, love each other, or choose each other. Love is a grave mistake, punishable by death. The unruly are killed, in cold blood. The massacre of lovers, or of one of them (always and without exception the woman), initiates the never-ending process of vendetta between clans.

Young girls are the articles of exchange and it is the tribal politics of inter-clan relationships that decides their marriage. The personal feelings of the young people concerned do not enter into the picture. This is why in *landays* the perpetual song is a cry of separation. Either the lover has left the country to make a living elsewhere or he remains in the village, but the social restrictions do not allow him to join the woman he loves. Her father and brothers are there, fierce and incorruptible guardians of the order. The woman suffers even more intensely from two kinds of misalliance—frequently her husband is either a child or an old man. It is this companion, forced upon her, whom she refers to as the "little horror." There is not a single *landay* that attests to conjugal love or to feelings of tenderness and faithfulness where the husband is concerned. Love and faithfulness are reserved for the lover.

This is how one woman evokes these two forms of misalliance:

Fate brought me as husband a child I must raise
But, God, when he is tall and strong, I shall be old and
weak.[1]

*

Cruel people, who see how an old man leads me to his
bed
And you ask why I weep and tear out my hair!

Even the monotony of life does not help her to tolerate such an ill-matched conjugal life with indifference:

Oh my God! Once again you send me the dark night
And once again I tremble from head to toe, for I must
get into the bed I hate.

---

1 In the *landay* form, though incomplete in meaning, this might be translated as follows:
Fate brought me as spouse a child to raise (9 syllables)
God, while he grows tall and strong, I age and I grow weak (13 syllables).

Oh Lord! Once again your long and dismal night is here
And once again he is here, too, my "little horror" and
he sleeps . . .

The "little horror" sometimes gets what he deserves, however, as in these:

My love, jump into bed with me and do not fear,
If it should break the "little horror" is there for the
repair.

*

When you come to our house, my love, the "little
horror" grows angry.
Don't come again. Hereafter I will give you my mouth
between the double doors.

However, in the area of love the belligerent woman expresses her feeling of revolt in a far more eloquent way. In a social milieu in which any mention of passion and sexuality passes for absolutely taboo, she is not afraid to touch upon these themes without beating around the bush and with brutal frankness. A human being of flesh and blood, she is proud to exalt her body, carnal love, and the forbidden fruit. She behaves as if she would gladly shock and scandalize men, while provoking them in their very virility. What confers a special power upon this discourse is the fact that there is no feeling of affection or pity mixed in with this.

That a woman should so loudly proclaim her love compels social scandal:

I love! I love! I shall not hide it. I'll not deny it.
Even if that's why you with your knife will cut off all
my beauty marks.

*

Last night I was close to my lover, oh evening of love
not to return again!
Like a bell, with all my jewels and deep into the night,
I was chiming in his arms.

*

Put your mouth on mine
But leave my tongue free to speak to you of love.

*

My mouth is yours, devour it and be not afraid.
It is not made of sugar that might be dissolved.

*

Tomorrow those who hunger for my love will be satisfied
For I want to cross the village with my face uncovered,
    my hair in the wind.

*

First take me in your arms and hold me tight,
Then turn my face to you and kiss my beauty marks
    one by one.

*

Come close to me, my love,
If modesty keeps you from touching me then into my
    arms I'll pull you!

Is there not a single madman in this village?
My pants, the hue of fire, are burning on my thighs.

*

My lover wants me to kiss him in the foliage of the
   blackberry bush,
And I leap from branch to branch to offer him my
   mouth.

*

Already the accursed rooster and his sad departure song
And my lover leaving like a wounded bird.

Yet, if the Pashtun woman invites the man to loving, she never appeals to him with her tenderness or sweetness. She provokes him in his honor and his dignity, but in this intrepid game it is she who takes the greatest risks. For the man can defend himself, flee, seek refuge in a distant land, while the woman has no such recourse. If she is discovered she can only let herself be slaughtered. Nevertheless, haughty as she is, she will not make any allusion whatsoever to the obvious danger that lies in wait for her. She is content only with encouraging the man, the brave warrior, to take a few risks.

By your side I am beautiful with my mouth extended
 and my open arms,
And you, like a coward, you let yourself be rocked by
 slumber!

*

If you are looking for the warmth of my arms, you will
 have to risk your life,
But if you prefer your celebration, then kiss the dust
 rather than love.

*

Come and kiss me without thinking of the danger.
 What does it matter if they kill you!
True men always die for the love of a beautiful woman.

*

Give me your hand, my love, and let us go into the
fields
So we can love each other or fall together beneath the
blows of knives.

II

WORDS SUCH AS these, that are to the game of love what the call to killing is to the art of war, openly deny the values permitted by Pashtun society. They imbue the virile consciousness with difficulties and discomfort, undermine his rights and his arrogance. For, since the life of the tribe is basically regulated by the honor code, the provocation that the *landays* contain functions like a dreadful trap. Since the main sanction of the code is that it cannot change, woman will strive to exacerbate its logic. From this perspective, her songs are original echoes of the master–slave relationship or, speaking poetically, of the cries of the persecuted-persecutor.

What actually is the woman's attitude toward the honor code of the male society as seen through the *landays*? In listening to them, we think we can hear a huge burst of laughter—a metallic laughter, cutting, reverberating, pitiless, and without affection. These tough and severe men seem like kids to her. It is almost as if she were speaking to these bearded children, saying: "Since you are so proud of your virility and so much love to play the game of honor, well then, I'll participate in your game and I'm going to make you shoulder the extreme consequences of your own principles."

Things occur as if this submissive woman, just an object among many others, an object of social exchange and above all the central object of the honor code, were by some dialectical irony becoming a subject, a resolve. In the arena run by men and for men, she seems to be taking things in her own hands and inverting the situation. With the help of her melodies alone, she decides to escape from the male who saw her as his property, as his commodity, and who believed he could do with her as he saw fit.

Thus, when an armed conflict erupts, the man really must leave; he cannot stay behind for the village girls will ridicule him. If he comes home from a battle, a long journey, or some exploit or other, he will inevitably wonder what the village women will say. If he comes back humiliated—beaten in war, for example, without having killed his rival, without having won enough material wealth with which to purchase some land, increase his prestige, or re-occupy a lost social position—it will be impossible for him to live honorably in his own home. His silent wife will look upon him with implacable scorn, her gaze eloquent and sarcastic, apparently obedient but cool and aloof. Finally, the reversal will be complete—it is the woman's opinion and her look that will decide how man, according to his own honor code, is to behave.

Furthermore, the Pashtun woman accepts the inordinate consequences of her attitude even where her own children are concerned. It is she who sends her son to a vendetta war, who advises him to conduct himself like a hero even if that means he will not come back alive—and if he does return but is wounded, he must show that his injuries are on his chest, not on his back. On the other hand, when she learns that her son has died on the field of honor, one has the impression of being in the presence of someone with full control over her feelings and free of any maternal "weakness." One can undoubtedly corroborate that she does, indeed, not feel what is normally called "motherly love" in any ordinary way. She appears to be shaped differently; her emotions are just as deeply human as any other emotion considered to be human but her psyche breaks away from the usual norms. This woman does not love the boy she calls her son with a "maternal love." She does not see the "fruit of her womb" in him, but rather a man who already belongs to the male community, to the opposing camp. Three reasons can explain such an extraordinary reaction:

1. Of all the slave labor that she performs the most difficult and most painful has to do with the large number of children she must feed and raise. She will see more than half of them die at varying ages. Without mentioning the dehumanizing hard work, this so often repeated spectacle of dying children hardens her heart. Moreover, in her life that is permeated with violence, feelings of "tenderness" and "motherly love" seem like an unattainable luxury.

2. When he is barely adolescent, the son begins to beat his mother. These bursts of brutality and cruelty against the person who is his mother constitute an initiation of sorts into adulthood, a guarantee of toughness. The father watches these scenes in which the son confirms his virility with a kind of indifferent complacency.

3. In the final analysis, children are generally the product of a forced marriage, the multiplied doubles of a despised husband who always behaves like absolute master and tyrant.

Here then, referring to tricks diverting honor, are a few *landays* in which the woman traps the man in his own value system:

Go first, my love, to avenge the martyrs' blood
Before deserving the refuge of my breasts.

*

May you perish on the field of honor, my beloved!
So that girls will sing your glory each time they haul
    water from the spring.

*

Oh my love! If in my arms you tremble so
What will you do when a thousand lightning bolts
    flash from the clash of swords?

*

In battle today my lover turned his back to the enemy.
I am ashamed of having kissed him last night.

*

Come back to me, riddled with holes from a dark rifle's
    bullets,
And I shall suture your wounds and give you my mouth.

*

*My beloved! If you turn your back upon the enemy, do
    not come home again!
Go and seek refuge in a distant land.*

*

*May you be found cut to pieces by a trenchant sword,
But may the news of your dishonor never reach my ears!*

*

*With my own hands I have sent you off to die,
And then I climbed onto the roof to see you brave the
    first volley of guns.*

*

*Hurry up, my love, and quickly rise to the assault,
I have put my bets on you with the village girls.*

III

CONSTANTLY IN TOUCH with death, the Pashtun woman nevertheless sees this ultimate moment in a very specific way. It should first of all be noted that there is no trace of the word "soul" in her vocabulary, nor even of any substitute that might come close. The Arabic expression *rouh* and what it implies as a spiritual entity, independent of the body and superior to matter, can be found only in the *landays* composed by people of letters or the clergy. Women use the Pashtun word *sa,* which only means "breath." And "rendering the *sa*" indicates stopping the breath, expiring, the end of all breathing. Nothing more. Woman therefore seems not to be concerned with a soul, separated and separable from the body. She sings exclusively of the body's destiny and of that physical reality she gives priority to one element, the heart. It is the seat of feelings, joy and sadness, fleeting hopes and deep despair, and so much so that the word "heart" is often used as if to take herself as witness. With this device the singer creates her own double and directs the poetic discourse to herself. The heart is also personified at times. It is then compared to a bird, a ruin, a fountain of blood, and to a closed oven devouring its own flames.

Thus, it is especially with her own body that woman feels comfortable. She speaks of its fragile growth like a wild flower in the high mountains, of the intoxication of her yearning eyes, of the nectar of her lips, the heroes' reward, of her beauty marks that are like stars in the firmament of a serene face, of her hair the color of the night, of her breasts splendid as Kandahar pomegranates, and of her velvety thighs.

However, the more she thinks of this body and its power to love, the more sensitive she becomes to time's fleeing and the ephemeral characteristics of existence.

Quickly, my love, I want to offer you my mouth!
Death is roaming through the village and could carry
    me off.

*

My beloved, come and sit a moment close to me
Life quickly turns into the dusk of a fleeting winter
    evening.

*

My love, open my tomb and see
The dust that covers the sweet intoxication of my eyes.

*

Oh ruined tomb, oh scattered bricks, my beloved is no
*   more than dust*
And the wind of my lament carries him off far away
*   from me.*

True daughter of the earth, the Pashtun woman seems to think that death is a simple return to elementary things—to wind, dust, grass, water, and fire. The hereafter does not haunt her. There is not a single female *landay* that expresses either the hope or fear of another world. On the other hand, what rules her deep despair is not to have lived enough, not to have sufficiently felt her beauty, her youth, and the pleasures of love. What causes her to suffer is not in any way the anxiety over an unknown lot or remorse over mistakes that were made. It is rather the regret that she will be snuffed out with the hunger for earthly nourishment inside her never satisfied, the thirst for mere human happiness never quenched.

Without any illusions about a future life and certain that all love on earth is inescapably bound to failure and death, the Pashtun woman elevates herself through her songs to the level of a tragic heroine. Her destiny inscribes itself in an immense space that has been interwoven with prohibitions by the law of men. She also nurtures her image with what cannot be refused to her—the nature that surrounds her. She is simple and uncomplicated like the pattern of the bare plains. She is pure, limpid, and impetuous like the waterfalls of the rocky valleys. She is beautiful, imposing, and hard, like the mountain with the blue reflections of the Hindukush.

FORTY LANDAYS

1

In secret I burn, in secret I weep,
I am the Pashtun woman who can't unveil her love.

2

You were hiding behind the door,
I was stroking my naked breasts and you caught sight
*   of me.*

3

I will gladly give you my mouth,
But why stir my pitcher? Here I am now, all wet.

4

Oh springtime! The pomegranate trees are blooming.
From my garden I shall keep the pomegranates of my
*   breasts for my distant lover.*

5

At night the verandah is dark, the beds too numerous.
The tinkling of my bracelets will tell you where to go,
*   my love.*

6

First take me into your arms and hold me close,
Only then will you be able to join my velvet thighs.

7

Kiss me in the moon's sparkling glow,
In our tradition it is in brilliant light we give our
*   mouth.*

8

Come and be a flower on my chest
So that I can refresh you every morning with a burst of
*   laughter.*

With me you have done all you ever wanted,
Lay a veil over my face from here on in: I want to sleep.

Careful, hold on, do not be discouraged!
Like a flowering branch bowed across your head, I am
   here close to you.

May God prohibit you from any pleasure as you travel
Since you left me while I, as yet unsatisfied, was sleeping.

Oh my love beyond the mountains, gaze at the moon
And you shall see me waiting where I stand on the
   rooftop.

13

Last night you were sleeping in my arms
And now so far away from me how will you find any
rest tonight?

14

Of my bosom I have made a bed
And my exhausted lover has far to go to come to me.

15

The white light of dawn grows wider
And poor me, I am still trying to bring the sullen lover
some delight.

16

My lover cannot take a joke.
With my long tresses I struck him gently and suddenly
he bristled.

17

My lover wants to keep my tongue inside his mouth,
Not for the delight of it, but only to establish his steady
rights on me.

18

Have you with your white beard no shame?
You caress my hair and inside myself I laugh.

19

Never shall I take an old man as a lover,
He wastes the night just planning things and in the
morning calls himself robust.

20

One is dying of desire to see me if only for a moment,
The other throws me from the bed telling me he's sleepy.

21

I have braided my hair but it has come undone.
My traveling lover must be in danger. May God protect
*   him!*

22

What else can he do but behave like a hero,
Since I am putting the pillow of my white arms
*   beneath his head?*

23

Last night I had a dream:
I saw myself in bed, half reclining and half in my
*   lover's arms.*

24

Come quickly, my love, so I can give you my mouth!
Last night I saw you in my dream, you were dead and I
*   went mad.*

25

You would be a heap of ashes instantly
If I threw you my intoxicated look.

26

Intoxicated just because I smiled at you,
You'd be raving mad if I were to offer you my mouth!

27

Oh rooster, wait a little with your song!
I have just come into my lover's arms.

28

Brush the dark bangs on my forehead aside, kiss my
*   beauty mark,*
It is a fruit from paradise, a lucky charm for life.

29

Learn how to consume my mouth!
First place your lips on mine, then gently force my teeth
apart.

30

Last night I had a dream that has come true:
My timid lover took me in his arms in the bright light
of day.

31

I have only yielded you the privilege of my mouth,
Do not go looking for the knots of my waistband, it
will be in vain.

32

Gently slide your hand inside my sleeves,
The pomegranates of Kandahar have blossomed and
they are ripe.

33

My pants, the hue of fire, are slipping down my thighs,
My heart is telling me you will be there tonight or the
next day.

34

God, what are you doing to me?
The others are flowers burgeoning and you are leaving
me as a tight bud.

35

Come, my beloved, come quickly and be close to me!
The "little horror" lies in slumber and you may kiss me
now.

36

You wretch who did not come last evening!
All night long I stood alone, waiting on the rooftop.

37

Stretched out I want to take him into me,
But my lover is alarmed. He fears the "little horror"
*   might awaken.*

38

My lover rests near where the flowers are
And on him lies the dew of my most tender kisses.

39

Gather some wood and make a great fire!
For it is my wont to give myself in the bright light.

40

I used to have bracelets, I do not wear them now.
Hereafter I will join my lover unadorned, with naked
*   arms.*

IV

THE PREVIOUS PAGES—the study and choice of the *landays*—restore the Pashtun woman's face from before April 1978, before the destruction, the slaughter, and the terror. The communist coup d'état followed by the Soviet invasion devastated the country as never before in its history. Imprisonment, torture, summary executions, ransacked villages, and burning harvests seem to have obeyed a strategy of horror that aimed only at imposing a *pax sovietica* similar to the peace of cemeteries.

One example among thousands is the massacre of Kirala. Early in the spring, one evening in March 1979, a group of resistance workers attacked a government post near Tchaghassaray, the administrative center of the province of Kunar. The next day, all of Kirala's men were taken to the village square. Then the commander of the military base, a *khalqi*,[1] opened fire and ordered his officers to shoot into the crowd. Every adult male, a total of one thousand seven hundred, was killed in cold blood. The only survivors were women and children. Now the widows and orphans of Kirala live in a special area in a refugee camp in Pakistan. It is a place where, between

---

1 Member of one of the factions of the Communist Party in power.

mourning and madness, the silence is crushing, where not a single woman sings any more.

After the invasion of Afghanistan by the Red Army on December 27, 1979, the great demonstration of April 1980 was organized by women. Girls from the elementary and secondary schools of Kabul, students of the university, teachers, workers, and even homemakers and mothers went out into the streets heading for the government's palace. Russian tanks broke into the crowd and dozens were killed and wounded.

Nahid, one of the women who had coordinated the protest march, called out at the *parchami*[2] officer who had his gun on her:

"Hey you coward! Since you are incapable of defending your honor you are not a man any more. Here, take my veil, put it on your head and give me your weapon. We women will be better at defending this country than you are."

The officer fired and Nahid, mortally wounded, fell. Since then she has become the symbol of women's resistance and numerous *landays* have immortalized her name.

---

2 Member of another faction of the Afghan Communist Party.

The beautiful Nahid rose up and in her clear voice
   cried:
Rise my sisters! The motherland needs us for her defense.

Thus, in the course of the last nine years of war, Afghanistan has suffered the most barbarous devastation and the bloodiest massacres. Out of a population of sixteen million, four million fled to neighboring states. This is the highest number of refugees in the world, to which should be added some three million deported from the interior, that is to say all those who were transferred from one province to another or who came only to be compressed into Kabul. As for the dead, there are hundreds of thousands of them.

More affected than others by these forced moves of the population (stemming from the borderline position of their lands), the Pashtun went to Pakistan in enormous numbers. Most of them—men and women alike—who kept alive the tradition of oral poetry, especially that of the *landays*, survive in camps today. Poetic creativity has not been extinguished for all that; on the contrary, the dreadful conditions of their exile have given them a desperate and irrepressible impetus.

In the resistance and among the refugees the number of those who devote themselves to poetry has markedly increased. If they know how to read and write they print collections of their poems; if not, they sing them, record them on audiocassettes, and try to distribute them.

This is also true for the *landays* that are coming forth in great profusion, from both people of letters and the illiterate. The only thing that has changed is the hierarchy of the themes. Love and eroticism are praised less, while religious outpourings, the call to holy war, nostalgia for the ancestral land, the sense of honor, and the glorification of heroism dominate.

The women's *landays* from the period of exile followed the same direction. The essential difference is the lack of religious leitmotifs that are so obsessive and stereotypical among the men. By the same token, the inspiration has lost some of its lightheartedness, its irony, and its sensual boldness. The new female *landay* tends to emphasize the experience of distance more as a wrenching, a wound—the absence of the lover in battle, the absence of the native soil.

Thus, the woman in exile addresses the wind:

Breeze, you who blow from the mountainside where my
    lover fights,
What message are you bringing me?

And the wind responds:

The message from your distant lover is the smell of
    gunpowder
And the dust of ruins that I carry with me.

Whatever the subjects are that have been devel-
oped in the new songs, the war's dark wing and the
despair of exodus haunt the melodies. When it is a
direct question of exile and patriotic combat, this is
obvious; but even when the contemptible figure of
the "little horror" emerges, the link with the need
for struggle often comes through. Only passionate
love keeps the old flame intact—alive, rebellious,
free, or even libertarian.

Divided into four major thematic groups, here
are a few of the *landays* that have been spontane-
ously created in the camps today. They are the
wounded echoes of the great anonymous voice of
women.

Exile

My beloved, my sun, rise above the horizon and
    obliterate my nights of exile.
The darkness of solitude cloaks me from all sides.

*

Living in this land of exile is ravaging my heart,
May God let me return to the foot of my tall mountains!

*

It is springtime, here the leaves are sprouting on the
    trees,
But in my land the trees have lost their foliage under
    the hail of enemy bullets.

*

God, you may render me blind from here on in,
With my lover gone I have no desire to see any other
    face.

*

My friends, which of these two to choose?
Mourning and exile arrived at my door together.

Battle

My sisters, tie your veils around like waistbands,
Pick up rifles and go off to the battlefield.

*

On our native soil, the martyrs' drops of blood
Are the red tulips of freedom's springtime.

*

If you do not have a wound in the center of your chest
I shall remain indifferent, even if your back is riddled
*   like a sieve with holes.*

*

If you truly love me, my love, go off and liberate our
*   land!*
My exquisite and tender mouth will belong to you
*   forever.*

The "Little Horror"

The "little horror," oblivious to combat, sleeps quietly
*   beside me.*
The only one with a right to my bed is he who prepares
*   to die for our country.*

*

The "little horror" does nothing—does not make love,
*   does not make war.*
At night, no sooner is his belly full, he climbs in bed
*   and snores until the dawn.*

*

I leap into the river, the current doesn't carry me away.
The "little horror" is the lucky one, I'm always thrown
*   back on the shore.*

The "little horror" will not die of his own fever,
I've decided that tomorrow I shall bury him alive.

*

Open a crack in the wall and kiss me on the mouth,
The "little horror" is a mason and will know how to
    repair the hole.

Love

How did you come here beneath the full moon,
You, as tall as a plane tree, where shall I hide you now?

*

Come, my love, let me embrace you,
I am the fragile ivy that autumn will soon carry off.

*

May God let him be invited to our home!
I shall have him taste the tips of my pink lips.

*

If you did not know how to love,
Why then did you awaken my sleeping heart?

*

The other girls are starting with new loves,
But I am piecing the tatters of an old love together.

*

Midnight already and you are still not here.
My blankets are on fire and burning me all over.

*

My love, come quickly and appease him,
The horse of my heart has broken every bridle.

If the power of the *landays* remains complete, it seems that the improvisational gift endures at the cost of an ever more inhuman hurdle. For the Pashtun woman in exile finds herself deprived of all her tasks and prerogatives. Confined to the area of her tent, she is more and more concealed by the increased pressure of religious prejudices. She no longer has her fields to be cultivated, no longer has permission to go about with uncovered face, and she is no longer free to sing and dance at weddings. She begins to be like a fish that has been thrown out of the water and lies expiring on the shore, like a plant that has been ripped from the soil and lies withering in a burning sun.

As for the men, they hardly notice the women's distress. They see them as useful auxiliaries they brought along just like the camels, goats, or horses that constitute their property. Nevertheless, without their knowing or feeling it, the women have stopped belonging to them. They have left their hearts behind and their souls are still roaming the valleys of Afghanistan. Through extra suffering, through a redoubled mutilation, they once again manage to deceive their companions, to dispossess them from what they own, since they are no longer anything but abandoned human beings.

All at once hard and tender, cunning and naïve, violent and gentle, the Pashtun woman personifies absolute exile. She keeps her distance from her soul and survives as if cut off from her heart. She remains indifferent—except when it comes to patriotic battle—to the gesticulations of men and to the games of children. Her only wish is to go back just once to draw water from the village spring at the foot of the high snowy mountains.

The woman in exile never stops dying,
Turn her face, then, toward her native land so that she
*   may breathe her last.*

NINETY-THREE LANDAYS
OF EXILE

1

Great God of the exiled!
How long must life on these arid plains go on?

2

Tears are streaming down my face,
I cannot forget Kabul's snow-topped mountains.

3

My beloved, I have nothing to offer you,
Except the dwelling in my heart's heart that I build
    for you.

4

Now mountains are separating us,
Birds alone will be our messengers and harbingers their
    songs.

5

I have made myself beautiful in my worn clothes,
Like a flowering garden in a devastated village.

6

My lover prefers sky-colored eyes
And I don't know how to change mine that are the
    color of the night.

7

At midnight the memory of you is the only visitor
That tortures me and prevents me from sleeping.

8

Oh springtime of unquenched desires,
Go find those whose hearts are still intoxicated!

9

Your love is water and it is fire,
Flames are consuming me, waves are swallowing me up.

10

If my lover dies, let me be his shroud!
Then together we shall wed the dust.

11

What else can you do but fight?
Subjugated you will be nothing but the slave of a slave.

12

A martyr is like lightning that glitters and is then
  snuffed out.
He who dies at home does nothing other than defile
  the bed.

13

Dust for you, but never my mouth again:
You hid when the men went off to battle.

14

If the hour has not rung, death will not be coming.
Were the world afire, my love, do not be afraid.

15

Had I known the time of separation was to come,
All the way to the battlefield I would have held my
    lover's hand.

16

Go and fight in Kabul, my love,
For you I'll keep both my body and my mouth intact.

17

Oh memory of my beloved, you are my one true lover!
You do not abandon me, it's you who mollifies my heart.

18

Hold me tightly in your arms,
I have prowled around solitude's prison far too long.

19

Go to sleep inside my eyes,
My nights' insomnia has diminished me to dust.

20

Oh Earth! The dues that you exact weigh far too much,
You gobble up our youth and leave the beds deserted.

21

I grow crazier with each passing day,
When I pass the tomb of a holy man I throw stones at
*   it for all my unrequited wishes.*

22

My lover is Hindu and I am a Muslim,
It is out of love that I sweep the steps of a forbidden
*   temple.*

23

Come to me so I can touch you and embrace you,
I am the evening breeze that will die before the dawn.

24

Make yourself my father's follower,
He will teach you how to study, I will teach you how to
*   live.*

25

Make yourself a beggar and a fool, then come in search
*   of me,*
Nobody may bar the way to wandering religious men.

26

Last night was the strangest night,
In my lover's arms I was trembling like a leaf.

27

God, please let my youth go up in smoke!
Handsome and proud men kill each other over me—I
    am becoming murderous.

28

My love, swear that you will come to me
So that I can strew flowers on your path.

29

If you sleep you will have nothing but dust,
I belong to those who all night long watch over me.

30

The outlaws stripped everyone down to the bone.
I was plundered beneath my lover's chest.

31

Oh lute that I would like to see demolished!
It's me he loves, it's you that lies moaning in his arms.

32

My lover is the ornament around my neck.
I might go naked, but without my necklace, never!

33

My heart said this to me: "I have no role to play,
It is the eyes who, watching, made me fall in love."

34

To chain me down he takes charge of the chains,
But if he truly loves me the links will not be drawn too
  tight.

35

Let this rock crush me with its weight,
But let no aged husband's hand ever brush against me.

36

Young men, defend me, defend your very honor!
My father is a tyrant who throws me in an old man's bed.

Go away then, my friend, and travel well!
You were but one of many lovers and I'll find a
hundred more.

God, do not let any woman die in exile!
With her last breath she will forget Your Name so as to
think only of her native land.

At midnight when the world's at rest
Fear rises up in me: where might my lover be?

You have consumed my mouth but are not satisfied,
You fool, carry me on your back, I am prepared to
follow you!

Why do you come to me so seldom?
Have they chained your ankles down, have they nailed
*   your feet?*

To my lover I want to sacrifice it all:
The rose of my face, the hourglass of my waist, and my
*   lips so like the rubies of Badarshan.*

Leave the service of your master and be my loyal
*   follower,*
Your wages will be the kisses of my mouth.

My lover prefers well mannered garden flowers,
But I, wild tulip that I am, I shed my petals on the
*   endless plain.*

45

My love, capture me, embrace me!
Banishment is a river taking me away and drowning me.

46

Come be with me like jewelry around my neck,
I shall rock you on the domes of my breasts.

47

God, please rescue just that one!
Or else they'll say my lovers die because I bring bad
  luck.

48

Oh damned rooster, I would like to strangle you!
Had you not sung, my lover would still be in my arms.

49

Hold me tight and very close to you,
For the storm that will carry me far away is rising.

50

Come, my love, let us go to bed together,
My woman's dignity is being in your arms.

51

Come, oh love's great sorrow!
I invite even you to find refuge in my heart.

52

The rooster is already announcing dawn
While there is so much left to say, such passion to
  consume.

53

Look what your love has done to me:
I was an apple, beautiful and red, now I am yellow,
  dry like an old orange.

54

God, is this then a sin?
You created this world's garden and the flower that
  really pleased me is the one I took.

55

Put your lips on my mouth,
Like a vine shoot twisting along the soil.

56

I shall bend toward you with my entire body
Like a vine shoot that twists along the soil.

57

Be happy, my love, I shall take charge of our cares.
My heart knows sorrow well and will not succumb to it.

58

If you kiss my mouth, you must give me your heart.
Those who leave my bed leave their hearts as surety.

59

If I stare at you with such great insistence,
It is because in you I see the hint of my next lover.

60

My love, come quickly to subdue it,
The horse of my heart is running rampant.

61

Unless you are mad with love for me
You shall not taste the succulence of my lips.

62

Do not crush me in your arms,
The buds of my breasts are trembling with a tender
*   pain.*

63

"Little horror," take your rifle and kill me now.
As long as I live I shall not forsake my lover.

64

Hurry up, my love, if you want to delight in me,
The "little horror" is pounding the clay to block up the
*   wall.*

65

God, provide the "little horror" with an eternal sleep!
The smallest cat awakens him and he spies on me
*   incessantly.*

66

God, take this old husband away
Who stands guard over my nights and sleeps all day.

67

They tell me that the "little horror" have fled the face of
*   the earth.*
Yet, mine is very much alive and tortures me besides.

68

See the dreadful tyranny of husbands:
He beats me and then forbids my weeping.

69

Son, if you desert our war,
I shall curse everything and also the milk of my breasts.

70

Heroes are always alive,
Only traitors will perish forever.

71

God, burn the houses down
Of those who destroyed mine and dealt out death at
    home!

72

My whole mouth, all of it, is yours,
I will give it only to the conquering warrior!

73

My beautiful lover, one day you will be killed,
And halfway there don't offer me flowers any more.

74

My courage fails me when I grasp my water jar,
My lover following me in the light of day is mad.

75

Do not hold me too closely in your arms,
Tomorrow the scent of my necklace will give our secrets
away.

76

Just to see you I invent circuitous walks.
Like a peddler I cry at every door.

77

Oh for the love of God, sleep, don't let it come to this!
This is the first night promised to my lover and I want
to be lively.

78

All my hotheaded lovers will be pleased with me,
I am not one of those who bully men in love!

79

I disgraced myself in my lover's eyes,
The night had barely fallen when I crawled into his
bed unbidden.

80

Pick the flowers by the handful,
I am a garden that knows that it belongs to you.

I have repainted my beauty mark and blackened my eyelids,
From now on when you look at me your reason will be forever lost.

One time only, just one time hold my bosom against yours,
And my loving heart will tell you its story.

My lover was dozing on armfuls of flowers,
And I, like morning dew, came down over him.

Either I want you on my bosom always,
Or else I would rather you be in the dark arms of earth.

85

Come onto my pathway one more time,
Your footprints are already fading in the dust.

86

God, you may render me blind today!
I want to see no other face: my lover has departed!

87

In the dark night that keeps us apart,
With a torch in my hand, I try to find my way.

88

Let the mullah raise his prayer to the dawn,
As long as my lover wants, I shall not get up!

89

God, let me be with him if only for a moment,
Like a fleeting lightning flash in the clouds' dark arms.

90

No longer will I draw water from the spring at dusk,
My lover is a demon who wants to possess me.

91

The others dress up in their new clothes for the feast,
I keep on the dress that still carries my lover's scent.

92

I have a fading flower in my hand,
Don't know to whom I'll give it on this foreign soil.

93

Bracelets on my arms, jewelry around my neck,
I'm leaving with my beloved, we are going home.

AFTERWORD

The Midnight Guide

––––––––––

by André Velter

I

A WINTER IN KABUL

IT WAS TO be my last trip to Afghanistan, but I did not know that. The plane was en route on its leg to Tashkent. Clouds were covering the deserts of Uzbekistan. The cabin was shaking in the turbulence of huge air pockets. Where we landed was not Tashkent.

You might have thought the airport was no longer in use. Potholes in the runway, broken windows, and dozing vagrants on the wooden benches. For a moment I thought we had crossed the border, but no, this was not Mazar, nor Kunduz, nor Maïmana. Some Cyrillic letters on the front of the main building confirmed the fact that we had not yet escaped from the Soviet grip.

It was then that I noticed his dark shape. He was standing with his back against the wall, facing the sun. His left arm was leaning on a cane, which emphasized the curve in his lower back and intensified the way he held his head. He had a wide forehead and rather long, disheveled hair. He was alone, standing by himself and, his eyes looking in the distance, he seemed to be smiling. His bearing was proud.

It was he who told us where we were—Dushanbe, the capital of Tajikistan—and why we were here: there was a sandstorm over Tashkent. He had not waited for any direct question but was already providing answers. He spoke superb and extremely fast French. He was coming back from Moscow after a tedious colloquium. It had bored him to death. Perhaps there was snow in Kabul? An early November snow. He had just started recounting a few earlier stays in Montpellier and Paris.

Some local men, dressed mostly in the long quilted coats of the horsemen of the steppes, were coming toward him one by one, not really hiding, saying a few words, and then handing him bits of paper. I thought they were all taking advantage of our unexpected, hence uncontrolled, stop to pass on some messages, to Uzbek or Tajik cousins from Afghanistan for example, or to uncles in Arabia.

"They are only giving me their addresses," our unknown companion said. "They want me to send them copies of the Koran!" And then he added cheerfully: "Sixty years of revolution just to get to this point. It isn't even the beginning of the end, it is as if the beginning hadn't gotten started—going nowhere.

Sixty years of stupidity and murder only to go back to the old tyranny of rock solid certainties!"

Once we were back in the plane again he was no longer within our line of vision. Serge Sautreau and I shared our exhilaration and surprise. This character was not easy to pin down. Grand, ironic, fiery, and seductive. Too natural to be a minister. Too candid to be an ambassador. Too much linguistic voracity to be an engineer. Therefore an intellectual, no doubt, but what kind? Archaeologist, historian, philosopher? Certainly not a businessman or a merchant. Obviously, the cheerful Afghan was beyond the norm. He had intrigued us right away.

Upon arrival he stayed behind on the gateway, slowly descending the steps. In the arrival hall, a swell of luggage thrown down in a jumble left us at some distance from him and we were forced to wave a silent goodbye. I was in a hurry to get back to the house in Kabul. The snow had not yet started falling.

A barely sketched description was enough for Emmanuel Delloye to identify our unknown figure and say without reserve: "That is Bahodine!" followed immediately by his first quality, "He is a poet, a very fine poet. They know him here as the white wolf." Emmanuel was astounded that I had never run into him before. In order to prove how totally unbelievable this was, he began in typically Afghan fashion with a series of family relationships that were, in fact, known to me: "He is the uncle of Zalmaï and Walid, Salahudin's brother, and therefore the brother-in-law of Shirin who also writes poetry herself." The result was that two days later we were sitting around the table in one of the Kabul apartments of the Majrouh clan and Bahodine was there.

In the meantime, his nephews, who for two years had been accompanying Marie-José and me when we were exploring the bazaars, had outlined the rather chaotic life and career of the poet for us. His full name was Sayd Bahodine Majrouh. He was born on February 12, 1928. His family originally came from the region of Kunar, north of Jalalabad, halfway to Nuristan. His grandfather, Sayd Hazrat Shah, was a highly respected man, and venerated as the spiritual leader of the Sufi brotherhood of Qaderia. His father, Sayd Shamsuddin Majrouh, a writer in both Pashtun and Persian, had been a minister, assistant prime minister, and an ambassador from 1940 to 1973.

But the child Bahodine had not had any right to be in the palaces of the capital city or the chancellery. He was raised in the mansion, made of earth, at Chinkorak and educated in a traditional Koranic school. He had only come to Kabul to pursue his secondary studies at the Lycée Istiqlal, the Franco-Afghan school where in 1950 he obtained his Baccalauréat in Philosophy[1] with highest honors. Then, on a grant from the Afghan government, he went to various European universities—Paris, Montpellier, Marbourg, Munich, and London.

Zalmaï and Walid did not know exactly what degrees—Master's, Doctorate—he had acquired but they did confirm that he had completed his itinerary and "very honorably" so. Back in Afghanistan and with varying degrees of success, Sayd Bahodine Majrouh had been a professor and dean in the Department of Letters of Kabul, governor of the province of Kapiça, president of the Historical Society, and chairman of the Department of Philosophy and Social Sciences at the University, a post he still held at this time in late 1977.

---

1 The *Baccalauréat* is the diploma earned after successfully completing the French *Lycée* curriculum. It alone provides entry to the university (translator's note).

These were a great many official titles for the dinner guest before us, who spoke with the same ease as he drank. Majrouh was quite ironic about his own interdisciplinary trials and tribulations.

"With a diploma in psychology and a thesis in philosophy, I was first urged to go in the direction of literature and history. Then the king wanted to nominate me to the governorship! From a distance, this may seem like an important position that allows one to take action and to change things. In reality, all you do is curb minor offenses and mediate insignificant conflicts. After six months I'd had enough of being pulled from my bed in the middle of the night just to settle the affairs of chicken thieves. I resigned. The king, holding no grudges, sent me off to Munich to head the Cultural Bureau of Afghanistan in Europe. I stayed there for four years."

In the end, however, the most important event was a car accident in 1972 that crushed one of his legs. There was no title and no honor whatsoever that could make up for no longer being able to run, climb, and walk any real distance. Even if it did not prohibit him from limping elegantly. At age forty-four, he woke up in a hospital bed with the near certainty that he would leave there a disabled person.

The blow that fate had dealt him would turn out to be a stroke of luck. All the more so as, month after month, one operation after another, while his bones were healing, the outcome appeared to be less dark—the shortened leg would leave him able-bodied. As he waited, the forced immobility obliged him to be truly in quarantine, for forty weeks rather than forty days. Society life, futile matters, and social rituals had come to an end. What he did have were solitude, physical pain, and time to get in touch with himself.

Professor, governor, and civil servant were false identities suddenly erased. Bahodine stopped being an ambivalent writer and an episodic essayist only to realize himself fully as a poet and philosopher. Besides, an act as completely accidental as this one revitalized the event that had given the family its name. *Majrouh* actually meant "injured" and the name was given as a patronymic to an ancestor who had been the victim of a very serious fall while jumping over a ravine. He had, however, survived the contusions and fractures. Over and above the name's meaning, Bahodine had found his very voice, his breath, and his light in an injury.

After dinner at Sahudin's and Shirin's, the evening continued at the house of Shar-î-Nao. The conversation took a political turn. Everyone was equally critical of the Prince-President Daoud, although none of the opinions concurred, nor did anyone offer an outline of what might lie ahead. To one person, violently bemoaning the general corruption, Bahodine replied in a semi-jocular, semi-serious tone: "Sure, those presently in power are much too corrupt, but I wouldn't want to see it replaced by a government that is too honest. With authoritarian regimes—and democracy is not going to come here any time soon—there should be a reasonable dose of ingenuity. It provides a little breathing space. Nothing is worse than those who are supposedly incorruptible. They stifle you with their principles, if they don't chop off your head right away. In a country where there is no freedom, it's not unimportant to be able to buy yourself some bits of liberty, even if it is on the black market."

Snow was late in coming. The cold was dry and biting, and in the cloudless sky the sun was almost friendly, the light magnetic. Bahodine came by almost every evening. If the group was small enough he quickly became the center of attention. He would sit at an angle on the sofa, his cane against his rigid leg and he'd lead the discussion. His voice was always cheerful. There wasn't any subject, even if it was serious or downright tragic, that would make him morose.

If a larger number of people were present, Bahodine, glass in hand, seemed to take pleasure in silently examining the incredible group that chance and the hospitality of Isabelle and Emmanuel Delloye had brought together. It was without a doubt the only place, the only no man's land in Kabul, of unadulterated conviviality. Members of the royal family were rubbing shoulders with communists of every feather, wealthy merchants were daydreaming next to a poor barber who'd hand them a joint, secondary school students would argue fiercely with university professors, while diplomats were telling embassy stories to exhausted archaeologists. There was also an authentic Sufi, a Dominican priest, travelers still suffering from jet lag, musicians, and occasionally the four silent sons of a great Kirghiz chief.

Bahodine was very much at ease in this mixed gathering, without any ceremony or constraint. He knew it was fleeting, illusory, and was well aware that a hundred yards away from this house the majority of those present would refuse to recognize each other. The importer of electric fans wouldn't greet the barber, the Maoist would only accuse the king's nephew, and the women would just look at their feet or remain anonymous beneath their veils. In the past, as governor of Kapiça, he had tried to break this social stranglehold, this form of segregation. Above all, he had tried to put an end to the impunity of the powerful in matters of justice. One episode in this battle was still famous.

A family of peasants had presented itself at the palace to condemn the intrigues of an *arbâb,* a village chief who was confiscating the water in the whole valley to his own advantage. These paupers were accusing an important personality, a great landowner, and, just to make the cheese more binding, a cousin of the Minister of the Interior. After listening to this at length, Majrouh invited the plaintiffs to his house while he used the time to verify some of the information. He sent someone he trusted to the area. The man returned a week later to confirm that the grievances were well founded. Majrouh summoned the petty tyrant, ran through the list of his abuses, forced him to compensate his victims, and finally, before the baffled peasants, had him thrown into the swimming pool at his house. "I could never have had him tried, much less sentenced," Bahodine observed. "All that was left was public insult, which is worse than prison."

One evening when we were together with just a few people, Bahodine opened one of the files he often carried around with him. It contained photocopied publications and a whole stack of handwritten pages—they were his complete writings as he had them at that time. Before giving any reading, he invoked the region of his childhood, near the Kunar River between Jalalabad and Nuristan. He endlessly insisted on the violence of life, the debts of honor, the vendettas, and the suffering of women. It was the first time that he spoke the word *landay*. He explained how, together with his sister, he had collected these very short songs—just two lines of nine and thirteen syllables each—in the Pashtun valleys. Then he introduced a set of them in a French transcription. I had never heard anything so glorious— laments like relentless challenges, cries hoarse with blood, mad passions that were trapped, inhuman destinies already doomed.

Then Bahodine began to read the poems and fables of the vast narrative cycle he was in the process of composing around the *Voyageur de Minuit*, his emblematic hero. From time to time, Sher would slip around us to fill the teapots. The metal of the wood stove was burning red. Outside the snow was falling in thick flakes. Bahodine couldn't be stopped. He gave himself over to an unpublished work that was visibly stimulating him, reading alternately in Persian and then giving a French version that he improvised on the spot. When he closed his thick notebook it was almost dawn. The silence that fell was rare, profound, overwhelmed, joyous, and magical, and nobody wanted to break it. Then Bahodine left, with his deep laughter, as if to excuse himself.

Without having consulted each other, Serge Sautreau and I decided right away to do everything we could to have the work we had just heard published in France. The next few days we sealed a kind of pact with Bahodine. He committed himself to providing us with a word-for-word translation of all his texts and we took it upon ourselves to "run them through the refinery," as he put it, before publishing them. It was early February 1978, and still fully winter in Kabul that year. There was no sandstorm over Tashkent. I expected to come back again before the summer.

II

EXILE IN PESHAWAR

Two months later, the Communist coup d'état, which had been planned in Moscow, would gradually immerse Afghanistan into a never-ending nightmare. Bahodine, whose epic grew to be more prophetic by the minute, perceived the immediate dangers, accepted the first clandestine tasks of the resistance organization at the university, and yet did not delay sending us the careful transcription he had promised. The mail, which more and more frequently arrived by diplomatic pouch, would deliver a bundle of handwritten pages with great regularity.

At the same time, however, there were long periods of silence as the correspondence was interrupted for months on end and we were uncertain about the fate of our friend. The most tragic events, from a distance at least, could have absurd repercussions, too. Thus, having submitted to *Temps modernes* a fragment of what henceforth was entitled *Ego-Monstre* in July 1980 for a special issue on Afghanistan, Serge Sautreau had taken the simple precaution of choosing a pseudonym for Majrouh to protect him from the torturers of the new regime in Kabul. They had decided to give the poet the name of a famous kite flyer who had been dead for ages and ages—Mosteri Baz Mahmat. As it turned out, the mask was quite pointless since Bahodine, helped by the resistance and under highly risky conditions, had managed to flee to Pakistan. When the review appeared in Paris, he had been in Peshawar for more than six months!

As soon as he was in exile, Majrouh created the Afghan Information Center, separate from any political organization, which thereafter published a monthly bulletin in English and a quarterly report in French devoted to the situation inside his country. He also pursued his personal writing with heightened energy and increased his trips abroad. Every autumn and every spring he would show up unexpectedly in Paris, his voice breathless and joyful on the phone, wanting to have dinner, which he'd squeeze into a hellish schedule. He kept up the transcriptions year after year without worrying about the publication delays we were running into.

In its November 1983 issue, the review *Nulle part* printed a superb version of *L'acheminement des humains vers le rendez-vous* (*The Consignment of Humans to the Appointment*) that he had completed with Serge Sautreau, thereby unveiling Sanâ'î, the poet from Ghazna who, in the twelfth century, had composed a kind of Persian *Divine Comedy.* One year later, the same review accepted the first set of *landays* we had translated together. The reception of these anonymous songs and the surprise their sudden inspiration provoked were reason enough to envision a separate publication. Each time Bahodine was in Paris, we would talk about the planned book and about *Ego-Monstre*, which Bahodine kept "running through the refinery." As we'd bid each other farewell, he would say laughingly that maybe we wouldn't see each other again. The situation in Peshawar was growing more and more tense, the hold of the Islamists over the refugees more and more harsh, oppressive, and threatening. He said that he was one of the designated targets.

In November 1987, Bahodine showed up again for just three days. He was at one and the same time seriously preoccupied, without any illusions, and careless. Only he could show such offhanded perceptiveness. He confided the specifics of his suspicions to me but without insisting, and urging me to take things lightly. He reserved his bit of melancholy for Paris, which the autumn bathed in a golden light. Suddenly on the Boulevard Saint-Germain he stopped, turning his head up almost completely and taking some very deep breaths. When I saw his face again, he was lively and bright once more.

I took him back to his hotel, close to the Gare de Lyon. Before getting out of the car, he repeated the ritual formula about the ultimate farewell. I answered and joked that I'd been hearing that for seven years now. We kissed each other. A wave of the hand before he opened the door. He was bubbling with life. Smiling, I drove off.

On the evening of February 11, 1988, Mike Barry told me about the murder. I let Serge know. Later, I wrote a small piece for *Le Monde*, entitled "The Assassinated Poet."

Afghanistan had just lost its greatest poet. In order to understand the dimension of the crime, one has to refer to the fate of Federico Garcia Lorca, like Sayd Bahodine Majrouh a victim of the same obtuse forces. Yesterday, it was an execution squad at the break of day in Grenada. Today, programmed killers in Peshawar, Pakistan.

Before being a philosopher, historian, professor, resistance worker, before being the tireless disseminator of information about the war imposed upon his country by the Soviets, Sayd Bahodine Majrouh was first the author of an immense work, an endless epic that recounts the wanderings of a lonely traveler who seeks the "ultimate site of liberty." *Collected under the title* Ego-Monstre (Ego-Monster), *these cycles of tales bear witness to a desperately prophetic perspicuity, whether they were written in Kabul or in exile.*

In his walk toward the rising Sun, the Voyageur de Minuit (The Midnight Traveler) *never ceases to run into the abyss that a tyrannical monster has chosen as its lair. He wants to warn, awaken, shake up the sleeping city, but its gates remain shut. An expatriate, he haunts the refugee camps and cannot silence his rage when faced with the fate reserved for women and lovers—he becomes an exile from the land of exile.*

Extraordinarily condensed, this overview of the work, nevertheless, does suggest what a free spirit Sayd Bahodine Majrouh was. His study devoted to the popular poetry of Pashtun women proves that he truly was an "enlightened man" *who obeyed the double heritage of the Sufi and the philosophers, a man who surely fought for the independence of Afghanistan but also for a new and future regime that would respect individual liberties.*

His assassination is the terrifying sign that an alliance has been forged between different forms of fanaticism, where the Communists prefer to yield their place to extremist Muslims rather than to have to move aside for those who are capable of reinventing a harmonious land. Majrouh could have pursued a brilliant academic and writing career in the West. He decided to remain, at all costs, with his own wounded people. He knew everything about the danger into which he branded his life; in the first stanzas of Ego-Monstre *he wrote:*

Throughout a whole long life of wandering across
oceans and plains, valleys and mountain tops,
I have scoured and crossed and seen some truths begin
to sprout.
With the first one, a road goes as far as the lost banks of
existence: it inevitably runs through
Hell

III

BAHODINE'S SECOND LIFE

The morning of the twelfth of February, the proofs of "our" book were in the mailbox. There was an additional injustice in this tiny delay. I added a short preface, a greeting to our friend, an "In Memoriam."

Sayd Bahodine Majrouh was assassinated as he opened his front door to people he did not know. It was the end of the afternoon, almost evening—the hour of dusk. The following day he would have been sixty years old.

He was alone and he knew the threat. He had never let anyone stand on the threshold. He remembered that at home, in Kabul, in Jalalabad or in Dar-î-Nur, the duty of a host would permit no hesitation. He died in a gesture of welcome, his chest torn to shreds.

He died for having spoken openly. He died above all for having listened to everything and having lent his voice to the voiceless. Majrouh did not in any way resemble an intellectual of the old school. He would rather hear the accounts and songs of a nomad, a shepherd, a peasant woman, or a madman of God than the perorations of a minister or a theologian. Without blinders on, he applied his erudition to questioning his own tradition.

This book, dedicated to the popular poetry of Pashtun women, gives a precise view of the magnitude of his independence of spirit and his daring. Dismantling as he did the puerile cogs in the wheel of the male code of honor, challenging hypocritical arrogance, buried oppression, conventional folly, this was celebrating the rights of the passion of love, of scandal, and of pleasure.

The heir of Omar Khayyam, Sanâ'î, Rumi, but also of Montaigne and Diderot, Majrouh ardently affirmed the profile of his unadulterated humanism. Having chosen the side of the Afghan resistance, he had no intention whatsoever of rallying the clan of fanatic bigots, nor of abandoning his mission as critical guide.

Indeed, his exceptional personality, his culture, his self-denial, and his brotherly fierceness were soon to appoint him the moral conscience of the resistance, while he was just as much its bad conscience, and explicitly so. Without any doubt, he saw too far and too deeply. Without any doubt, his insolence was too joyous, like that of those who know how to think, to act, and to transmute the darkness all at the same time.

As a poet, Sayd Bahodine Majrouh led an exemplary battle. He was committed on a daily basis, humbly, and without any weakness. Confronted with horror and barbarism, he himself did not in turn become a barbarian. He did not compromise.

Bahodine, you loved the seasons when the wind would rise and the sky would fill with magic spells and sand. You aroused the migrating entry of space so that heavy burdens would fade away and liberated hearts would be reborn. Bahodine, you were among those who are hurt by the fear of children but who are never alarmed by nothingness, the absolute, God, or the ultimate light. On the other side of the enigma, I wish you a bountiful dawn.

Songs of Love and War (*Le suicide et le chant*) appeared in March 1988 in the collection "Comme" under the direction of Bernard Noël at Cahiers des Brisants. During the years that followed, Editions Phébus published the complete *Ego-Monstre* in two volumes. The first one—*Le Voyageur de Minuit*—came off the presses at precisely the moment that on the side of the Hindu Kush the invaders were busy packing up to go. The opening article in the *Monde des livres* celebrated "Majrouh, the Watchman of Afghanistan."

Today, in the convulsive movements of the Soviet debacle, we can assess to what extent his ruined country lacks a personage of his stature and poised courage, how much it lacks a man without any craving for power, without any fanaticism, without any bigotry. As his great work comes out and Kabul is for the taking, we can also consider how cruel fate has proven itself to be: death stole both his book and his city away from him.

Yet, Majrouh's presence, the uniqueness of his voice, his role as watchman and messenger are now affirmed here in the bright light of day and for a long time to come. The publication in France of the first three cycles of Ego-Monstre *constitutes a decisive event, here as well as in the Afghan memory. All the more so because, by a well-nigh miraculous combination of circumstances, the book offers an almost complete version of the work even though the original itself is truncated. In fact, during his flight to Pakistan in 1980, Majrouh lost half his manuscript. Chance had it that only slightly earlier he had sent the word-for-word transcription in French to Serge Sautreau.*

The latter therefore completed this spellbinding transcription by himself and, as a poet, provided a superb version that is both dazzling and sober, harsh and lyrical. Thanks to him, The Voyageur de Minuit *enters into what is the "true legend" of our time. For, if Majrouh's hero "walks tirelessly through deserts and mountains, from city to city, in order to avert catastrophe, admonish vigilance in the face of the Monster, in the face of Tyranny," it should not be forgotten that these pages were written before the invasion of Afghanistan and that, over and above their obvious prophetic weight, they testify to a genius of universal premonition. It is really a question of visionary exhortation, of an epic that unites wonder and rebellion, song and the critical exploration of chasms. Where else have we read a more accurate decoding of the oppressive figure that—whether in Rumania or Chile, in Libya or Zaïre—imposes his viciousness?*

You know, oh Traveler, what happened and how the Monster found himself alone in his palace in the end, in the heart of a city without a soul, sovereign over an empire of nothingness.

Alone among the vaults and arcades, alone among the innumerable paintings endlessly representing him, the only image and central motif in every tapestry, alone with the paneling and crystal chandeliers always carved with the Dragon motif, he loved contemplating himself at length in the abundance of looking glass and mirrors with which he had furnished the palace and which reflected the exclusive shape of the Monster from every side.

It became harder and harder for him to turn away from the mirrors.

Without them he thought he would disappear.

Unaware of their threat, ignorant of their powers, he thus went to the gravest failure of his abominable existence.

He knew nothing about the magic of mirrors.

He did not know they are the threshold of the true night.

In Sayd Bahodine Majrouh's very writing, in the feverish compactness of his words, there is a swell that ceaselessly rises to the surface and comes to lift, remove, and intensify the tale. Then such lavish prose suddenly leaves its rhythms; it explodes, splashes, rustles, turns into a torrent, an undertow, the product of sound and meaning. By breaking and entering, out of a need for rupture, the story, the legend, or the fable becomes poem. Not a haughty, hieratic, blazoning poem, but a poem of movement, of fusion in which bursts of narrative, flashes of thought, lightning, and furor prevail. A poem that burns the stages and disperses the ashes of the inner path before it works its way back, quite naturally, to prose and the boundless wanderings of the Traveler.

> Then he knew.
> Never, from the depths of the horizons
> would the prophetic wanderer emerge, the traveler
> whose finger pointed at infinity
> at the incandescent goal,
> the transparent way,
> the inaccessible light.
> He knew then
> the only way,
> what he had to do,
> and which remained:
> go straight into the very den of darkness.

An inspired storyteller, Majrouh does not let himself be taken in. Like Henri Michaux, he knows how to treat a plot bluntly, change its perspectives, the angles of attack, taking both the prey and its shadow at the same time, and even in the middle of the desert, swap the sermon for terse language. Without denying his heritage, he has invented a new genre—the epic fable.

"The Rebellious Hymn of Sayd Bahodine Majrouh" was the title of the article I devoted to the second volume of *Ego-Monstre: Le rire des amants* (*Ego-Monster: Lovers' Laughter*) in May 1991. Before all else, what mattered was to affirm Bahodine's everlasting presence and to assert that his work was still effective and in force, even at a great distance from its original territory.

With his final text, Majrouh bequeathed an unforgettable book, a book of universal resonance that would be forever current, a lucid book guided entirely by the intelligence of the heart. It should be required reading in every church, mosque, school or army barracks, in every production workshop and in all the circles of power. Indeed, these pages contain the most forceful and stimulating antidote against tyranny, obscurantism, and each of their recurring subterfuges. What takes place here is the relentless decoding of the mechanisms of terror, while light is shed on manipulations, acts of cowardice, and denials.

Yet, it is really a narrative composed of a series of tales, fables, verse sequences, and not of a didactic essay. The "pedagogy" slips in almost by surprise, the moral comes in breaking and entering, and the thinking appears as if in a sudden revelation or a burst of laughter. Majrouh practiced Diderot as much as The Thousand and One Nights—*he knows how to philosophize on the way, to meditate though one wouldn't think it, to predict occasionally, to listen to children, and to love, always to love.*

Referring to him, Serge Sautreau quite rightly speaks of "Sufi modernity," thereby attesting to what extent Majrouh—in the midst of the prevailing sectarianism—compels recognition as a unique, singular, and audacious human being and how much he seems to be the equal of his hero, the equal of the Midnight Traveler. *The latter, who in the earlier book had done nothing other than announce the coming of darkness and infamy, here finds himself sharing the experience of exile with his author. It is an even more dizzying quest that begins, an even riskier expansion, and a more sorrowful downfall. The Traveler discovers that the shadow produced by the Monster—no matter what the identity he bestows upon himself: Dragon, Great Con-*

queror, or unrestricted Leader—knows no borders, and that oppression, hatred, and stupidity are equally at work among expatriates, exiles, and the uprooted. Thus, Majrouh describes the arrival of the fateful Messengers who, with sermon and dagger in hand, gradually ensure their hold over the camps.

Soon, the length of one's hair became law and whoever did not grow the indisputable and sacrosanct beard saw himself pointed at as a wicked man and a contemptible believer, unworthy of membership in the intransigent and immaculate brigade of the Enemy-of-Satan Brotherhood.

Progressively, the refugees ended up by allowing themselves to be subjugated by the virulent charm of the so-called doctors of the faith. Fine words in small gifts, mental and material dishonesty finished the job, and a majority of the exiled let itself be contaminated.

Obviously there was a hunt on the unbelievers. Those attached to their inner freedom were indicted. One had to be silent or else escape—or resign oneself to being kidnapped in the middle of the night. Obviously, there were those who disappeared for no apparent reason and murders without any assassins.

If the Afghan tragedy serves as a setting for the epi-sodes and intrigues of the book it does not constitute its entire framework. Majrouh has a sharp eye, fixed on detail, on the concrete signs of people and things, but he creates a broader plan. He invokes very precise desti-nies, easily recognized conflicts without ever mention-ing them by name, however, and thereby allowing their immediate passage to become emblem and myth. The title story, of the carefree and sublime lovers, un-folds in that time beyond time that seems to belong to age-old memory. The encounter of Delazad and Gu-landam thus appears as the simplest and closest thing to love at first sight. Everything about it is fortuitous, nec-essary, written.

We moved forward to meet each other, slowly, since the beginning of time. My whole life was going to make sense, I knew it . . . and I knew nothing at all.

Beautiful, to the extreme. With her clothes of old emerald, a color washed out by sun and wretched-ness, with those strands of hair fluttering across her forehead, with that enormous gaze suddenly riveted to mine as if it had been submerged there for eter-nity, she stirred up a forgotten source in me—very distant, very deep—a sensation beyond memory, and I recognized her, her whom I did not know.

This beginning and yet already absolute love, a love made up of bright light, enthralls the Midnight Voyager. He wants to believe in this force without shadow that measures itself only by joy, beauty, and life fervently lived. He listens to Delazad who reveals the secret of the free heart to him, the heart that, against everything and everyone, leaves itself free to love and laugh. The price of such lightheartedness, of such impudence, will be terrible: rounded up by the sinister Enemy-of-Satan Brotherhood, the refugees will arrive to stone the lovers. And the Midnight Traveler, the only one to come to their aid, crying out in horror and revulsion, will come to know a new exile amid the exiles.

Majrouh had witnessed a similar disgrace in Peshawar and it had left him with an incurable wound. Here he composes a defiant hymn, a furious lament that condemns and transfigures the murder of the innocent, and intimates where the agents of his own death will come from. Besides, it could go no other way for the one who cited as his model the wise man who professed that "Instead of consolidating faith, I awakened to research. Instead of reinforcing a reason, a principle, I pursued critical spirit, methodical doubt, and lucidity."

That is very much the stamp of Sayd Bahodine Majrouh—an intrepid and smiling lucidity, welcoming and irreducible, the lucidity that rips the masks off the Monster but does not omit the exploration of by what intimate acceptance, by what common vertigo despotism lurks inside everyone. What we have here, mingled in one single movement, are a metaphysical aspiration and libertarian upsurges, a savage mystique and a deep compassion.

Songs of Love and War (*Le suicide et le chant*), as it appears here vastly expanded, brings together all the *landays* that Bahodine collected in the valleys of Afghanistan and the refugee camps of Pakistan. Verse lines that resisted translation have suddenly, after many years, found their phrasing in French. This small book, as we know, was full of danger for its author. Today, Bahodine's assassins and their followers are at work all over the lands of Islam. May these songs of anonymous women bear witness to the enduring survival of a rebellious conscience, of impassioned memory, and of fierce refusal, in the very camp of the executioners. May their cries sound the alarm.

A.V.
(July 1993)

About the Author

Sayd Bahodine Majrouh was born on February 12, 1928 and assassinated in Peshawar, Pakistan, on February 11, 1988. He had obtained his Ph.D. in Philosophy from the University of Montpellier, had been Dean of the Department of Literature in Kabul, Afghanistan, as well as Governor of the Province of Kapiça. After the Soviet invasion, Majrouh went into exile in Peshawar where he founded the Afghan Information Center, which broadcast reports on and analyses of the resistance across the entire world. He was the author of a vast epic, *Ego-Monstre* (Ego-Monster), which constitutes the whole of the major poetic work of twentieth-century Afghan literature. Heir to Omar Khayyam, Sanâ'î, Rumi, but also to Montaigne and Diderot, Sayd Bahodine Majrouh's profile was an impassioned validation of the indomitable humanist. This is the portrait André Velter paints of him in the afterword, "The Midnight Guide."